Contents

Some words are shown in bold, **like this**. You can find them in the glossary on page 23.

What are the parts of a plant?

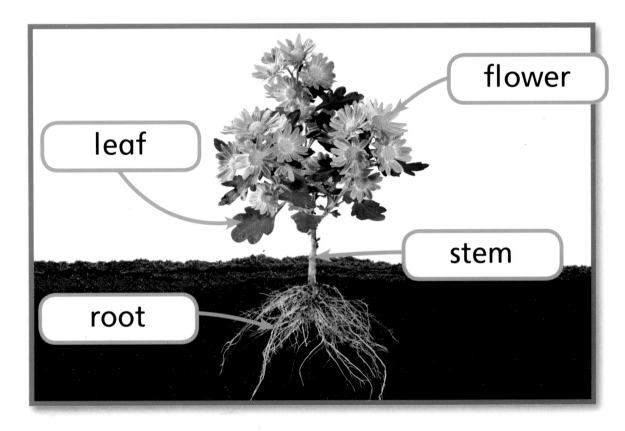

leaf

flower

stem

root

There are many different kinds of plants.

All plants are made up of the same parts.

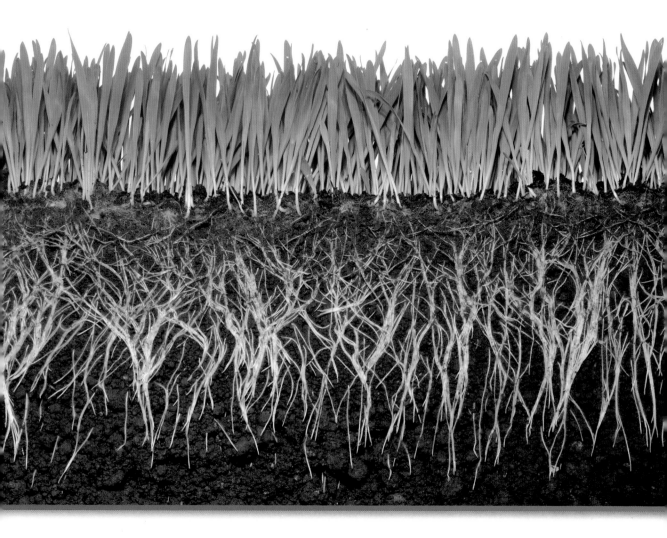

Some plant parts grow above the ground in the light.

Roots grow below the ground in the soil.

What are roots?

roots

Roots are plant parts that grow under the **stem**.

Some roots grow just below the ground.

Some roots grow very deep below the ground.

Water lily roots grow at the bottom of ponds and lakes.

Why do plants have roots?

root hairs

Plants need water to grow.

The **root hairs** soak up the water that plants need.

Roots also hold plants firmly in the ground.

Roots stop trees being blown down by strong winds.

Where do roots come from?

seed

root

Roots come from **seeds**.

The root is the first plant part that grows out of a seed.

leaf

stem

root

Roots grow downwards into the soil.

Then a stem grows upwards into the light.

How big are roots?

Roots come in many sizes.

These leeks have roots that are short and thin.

Some roots are long.

Mangrove roots are long and thick.

How many roots can a plant have?

Some plants have just one root.

Radish plants have one fat root.

Some plants have lots of roots.
This tree has hundreds of long roots.

What colour are roots?

Many plant roots are white, but roots come in different colours.

Beetroot and radish plants have red roots.

Carrot plants and sweet potatoes have orange roots.

How do people use roots?

People use some roots for food.

We sometimes eat carrot roots raw.

Sometimes we cook roots before
we eat them.

How do animals use roots?

Animals use roots for food, too.

Guinea pigs have sharp teeth for biting into roots.

Some animals shelter among
tree roots.

They make their homes among roots.

Measure and record

This bar chart compares the length of some different roots.

Can you see which plant has the longest root here?

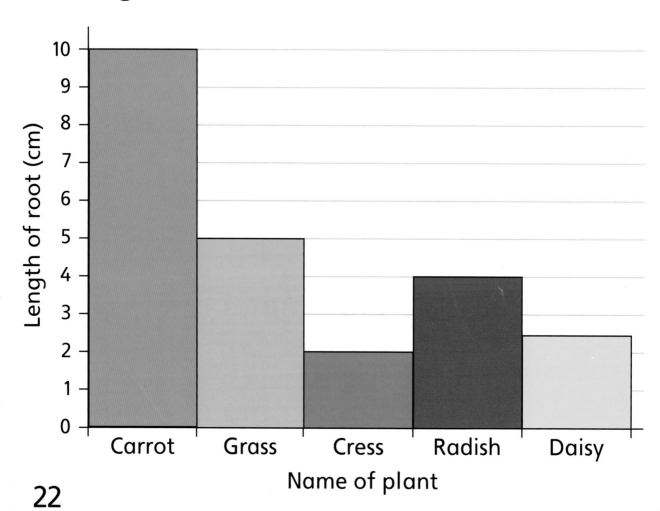

Glossary

 **root hairs** the parts of roots that are so small, they look like hair

 **seed** the part that new plants come from

 **stem** the part of a plant where the leaves and flowers grow

Index